How

Dealer

By [673126]

Disclaimer

The following information within this book is intended for entertainment purposes only. In no way does the author, publisher, or any associates thereof encourage, or condone any acts written within. If the reader chooses to recreate the scenarios discussed, he or she does so at their own risk, and assumes all liability for their actions.

Prologue

In today's America, we have seen the rapid decline of prosperity and the increase of unemployment. In the workplace, employees are given just enough wages to pay small portions of the debt they have racked up, without being able to afford benefits or even save for retirement, let alone vacation with their families.

Instead, we are expected to wake up, get dressed, go to work, come home, go to bed, repeat. On top of that, we are expected to take on credit cards to build a credit score that allows you to take on even bigger amounts of debt, like buying a home. We are expected to repay this debt with money that we spend hours and hours and hours away from our families to get! So this whole time you are out trying to earn money to pay for things you don't even get to enjoy!

Doesn't this seem stupid? Doesn't it seem more logical to spend more time at home with your family, or to actually *live* instead of just survive? In this world, we have seen the promise of the "American Dream" revoked, and we have been enslaved to a society that cannot seem to figure out its priorities. I offer you a way to change that...

Table of Contents

.

Chapter One:

Finding the Right Market

So you want to sell drugs... good for you! Drugs have been around for a very long time, and no matter what laws we pass, or the **millions** we incarcerate, drugs aren't going away. It's time to cash in on that.

You've been down this road before. You've questioned the politics of our Puritan America, and you've had many sleepless nights trying to figure out how to stop your car from getting repossessed. You always wondered how much you can actually make by selling drugs. You watched countless movies on the subject, admiring the man in the suit with the blood on his hands and the mountain of cocaine on his desk. But real drug dealers are nothing like the ones in the movies. **In this world, it pays to be humble**.

Just know that you are not alone in your decision. There are many drug dealers who currently operate, some of them low-level street dealers, but some of them are as powerful and rich as corporate board members. It, too, is a job with potential to advance. There are people just like you who are advancing their careers as you read this sentence.

Another thing I want you to know is that this does not make you a bad person. The term *drug dealer* has a very bad connotation to it that I want you to dispel immediately. Forget that derogatory term, *drug dealing.* Instead, call it "**hustling**", or "**illicit sales**".

You are no more evil than the convenient store clerk who sells people alcohol and cigarettes. You are no more evil than the small business owner that sells jewelry at the kiosk in the mall. You are simply, a business person. There is a demand for a product, and you are the kind soul who is risking freedom to supply a customer with that product they so eagerly demand. This does not make you bad, it makes you the epitome of the American Capitalist. **You are the CEO of your own enterprise**, and that enterprise depends solely on decisions you make.

That's right. **<u>You control your own destiny in this business</u>**. So long as you are not in gang controlled territory, you won't have to pay any taxes or answer to any organization like legitimate businesses do. However, if you do operate in a gang controlled territory, make sure you pay them your taxes and you don't step on any toes. That last place you want to find yourself is in the middle of a grape vineyard with your tongue pulled out from a hole in your throat. This does not usually happen, as most dealers are regular people just like you, who needed to catch a break.

So, you've weighed out the pros and cons, and you've made your decision. Now what? How are you supposed to get started? It's not much different from starting a regular business. First you have to know what to sell.

Check within your area, ask around, go to parties, and be social! Being social not only helps you to enjoy a fuller life by experiencing emotions with other humans, but it also allows you to **build a vast network of clients**.

Ask these potential clients what kind of stuff they are into. Most people are relatively honest about their vices when they are in comfortable situations. This can give you a good idea of what to sell. This doesn't mean pressure them, and be a fucking creep about it. You have to know when to ask about that kind of stuff. I couldn't even begin to tell you when the time is right. You just have to learn how to read social cues. So if you have Asperger's, sorry bud, but you're not cut out for this business.

If you watch the news, or search the internet for news sources, you will often see drug arrests highlighted. Notice what drugs are involved in the arrests. Most cases will either be methamphetamines, pills, or marijuana. Whichever is most popular in your area is what you're going to want to sell.

Whatever drug you decide, be cautious of your client base. Yes, you want clients, you love your clients, your clients put food in your mouth, but what kind of people are they? Meth tends to attract of type of client who doesn't care what time it is, which can lead to phone calls at 3:00 am. They also tend to steal to pay for their habit, which in turn puts you at risk of getting robbed. In a lot of cases, meth addicts have been arrested and turned on their supplier to escape incarceration.

These are things to consider when selecting a product. At the same time, don't be too afraid to sell something popular like meth. Don't be an idiot and try to sell "shrooms" because hardly anyone still buys them. Popular drugs like meth have big rewards, too. Because of their addiction rate and popularity, they sell much faster than other drugs. **This means you make much more money in an exceptionally short amount of time**.

From my personal experience, after my first stint in prison, I got heavy into the marijuana game. So while my examples may involve marijuana specifically, the principles apply across the board. I did have a hand in establishing a rewarding meth ring, but not until much later, which we will also discuss.

In California, marijuana is pretty easy to come by. The simple fact that it has recently been decriminalized makes it that much easier, however it tends to flood the market as well. More and more pot dealers are coming out of the woodwork, but that's OK. Use these ambitious salesman as part of your network.

Networking is key to success at anything you do, illicit sales are no different. You need to set your sights on a "connect", or a "hook". A connect is someone who has the supply of drugs. A connect can range from the street level salesman, to the farmer who grows the magical stuff. Your main goal right now is to get one.

The best thing to do is to either find a grower, or grow it yourself. I warn you that growing cannabis is not as easy as it seems, and requires a lot of work. So, for all intents and purposes, let's find you a grower.

Growers are not that difficult to find. You could meet someone in the Emerald Triangle (Humboldt County), or ask other dealers about their supplier. Most people won't give you that information, so you have to ask in a deceptive manner.

You can't ask the guy if you can meet his connect. It doesn't work that way. But you can ask your dealer friend if you can purchase more than he has in stock. Most low level guys stock anywhere from a quarter pound of weed to about two pounds of weed. Ask these guys if you can purchase five pounds of weed.

Most of these guys do not have that much on them, so they eagerly talk to *their* connect (hopefully a grower) about you. The whole time, they are focused on getting a cut of either weed or cash for hooking you up. Give neither.

You are only trying to meet with his connect so you can get a contact number. If the only way to get this person's contact information is to meet up with them and check out their product, then meet up with them. But don't buy anything yet.

Relax, it's not like in the movies. If you don't make a purchase, they are not going to tie you up in the woods and take a chainsaw to you. Meet them where it's convenient for them, and they won't be too upset. Just look at their product. Give them accolades for the quality of their product if it is warranted. Then, tell them you appreciate meeting with them, but you are looking for a different strain because you already have enough of whatever strain it is they brought you. Tell them you would like to have their contact info so that you can stay in touch to make a future purchase. They will oblige because even though you turned them down right now, they want your business in the future. If you're still afraid of wasting their time, you can always offer to purchase a sample from them.

A word of advice: Be cautious, because it may come across like you are an undercover cop. Try not to give this vibe. I know it seems impossible, because now you're going to focus on not looking like a cop, which makes you look like a cop. Just try to relax, keep eye contact, and do business where they choose. This gives them a better reason to trust you.

Now, you have a valuable connect direct from the source, and you didn't have to work your way up the chain like the other guys. You are already ahead of the program!

Depending on how much money you have to invest, you are going to make a purchase from that grower. The only real way to make decent money, is to buy as much as you can at one time. Just like in wholesale for legitimate business, the more you buy, the cheaper it is.

My suggestion would be to buy no less than a quarter pound, but if you can afford it, buy a pound. A pound of marijuana in California around harvest time, 2014, can run you about $1,000-$1,500. If you can swing those prices, batter up.

The grower will be excited to hear from you, and give you a good deal. Some people may claim that he will tax you, meaning he will charge you a little extra, because you didn't purchase the first time around. This is not true. Growers have people to buy their product all the time, and you not making a purchase that first time didn't affect him because he went a block away and sold it off anyways.

If you cannot get to a grower, that's OK. If you don't have $1,000 to invest, that's OK, too. There are other ways to get it. I started out with $30 of stolen money, and built my way up. I bought an eighth, 3.5 grams, of weed, sold each gram for $15, and did it over and over again until I had enough money to buy an ounce.

Believe it or not, you can go on Craigslist and find marijuana for sale in smaller amounts. Try to buy an ounce if you can. Most ounces of good weed sell for about $180-$220. Then you can sell it off by the gram. Sure, the profit margins are small, but over time you can build up.

Keep in mind that you do not want to stick to just one supplier. This does not mean that you should not be loyal to that supplier, but you want to diversify. If you stick to only one supplier, the flow may dry up, and they may run out of product for you to sell. The last thing you want is a client list that needs your services but you have nothing to sell them. Not only will you miss out on that particular sale, but by the time you *do* get new product, they will have given their business to another source. Now you've lost out on future sales as well. Diversify your supply while maintaining a loyal partnership. Not only will you be much safer when product becomes scarce, but you will also have different types of product to offer customers.

People love having options. Think about it, most department stores do not sell only *one* brand or *one* item. If you have multiple strains at different prices, a customer is more inclined to come to you and to stick around to try all your product. You will be like the department stores of drug sales.

Now you have your weed. How do you get customers? Surprisingly, customers will come to you in time, but for now you have to advertise a little bit. Obviously, you cannot just take out a billboard ad or run a local TV spot. So how do you advertise an illicit substance?

9

I suggest that you first make little business cards with **just your phone number** on it. No pictures, no names, no product listings. Make sure you have these on you all the time, you never know where a potential customer can be.

Remember that party I suggested you go to? This is the best way. Go to a party with a very nicely wrapped joint. If you don't know how to roll a joint, there are tutorials online. Take that amazingly wrapped joint filled with your best stuff, and announce to the partygoers you will be outside, enjoying some "fire". The stoners will follow.

Share that joint with them, making sure they get enough to get high. If this means you don't get to toke, then make the sacrifice. You don't want them to remember your joint as the one that didn't get them high.

After people start to pass it around, let them know that you have a lot more if they want to buy some. Give them that little business card and ensure them that you have plenty of the stuff they love.

If you are feeling rather risky, you may want to bring some product, along with your scale and baggies. Remember though, this is very risky. In most places, if you are caught with a scale or baggies, you will be charged with **intent to distribute**, and this is not good when you have to go to court to fight it.

However, the reward can be worth it. At one party alone, a salesman can expect to make a few hundred dollars at least within the first hour of operating.

If you have a day job, often times you will find that your co-workers are potential customers. Unless you work for a federal or even local government agency, drug users are abundant. Ask your peers in the workforce if they are interested. It goes without saying, of course, that you should be careful doing this. Make sure no one will snitch on you, and your boss won't find out.

Another place you can attract customers is through Craigslist. Believe it or not, you can find all kinds of vice industry services on there. If you are afraid of attracting unwanted attention, make an email account and only list that email on Craigslist. Just make sure you check that email regularly so that you don't leave customers without product.

In California, medical marijuana is permitted so long as the patient in question has a valid doctor recommendation. If so, you can advertise to those patients on Craigslist under a "Prop 215" listing title. Then all you have to do is verify that the patient does in fact have a doctor recommendation that is current and up to date. He offers you a "donation" for your medicine, and then you repeat the process.

If you are dealing hallucinogenic or "party" drugs, like MDMA, Ecstasy, or LSD, you will want to go to clubs and other commercial party venues. Raves are excellent choices to push your product, but the best way to sell product like that is to find a promoter, someone who gets people to party for a living. That guy will buy almost everything you have, week after week.

In most cases, customers will find you via their friends who bought from you. If you're an awesome, and friendly dealer who never gyps the customer, they will brag to their friends about you. "My drug dealer is so fuckin' awesome!" Word of mouth is really where advertising comes in. If they hear how amazing you and your product are from their friends, they *will* come to you.

If you are selling drugs like cocaine, heroin, methamphetamines, or even the unmarketable magic mushroom, offer some free samples. You know damn well what a meth addict looks like so it shouldn't be hard to find a market for it. Give a potential client a "bump" or just enough to get them high for a little bit. This will not only attract customers, but it can perpetuate an addiction, thus making you the person who's got the fix.

Finding the right market or tapping in to the right market depends solely on you. That is the beauty of this industry. You don't answer to some uptight goober who got bullied in high school and now he wants to take it out on you. You don't wake up at 6:00 am just so you can get to your lame ass cubicle and make someone else rich. You get to make **yourself rich**!

In review:

Know you're not a bad person. Look, we all fall on hard times. The difference between you and the next guy is that you are determined enough to not give up. When the only company hiring involves selling something illegal, what other choice do you have? Die? I didn't think so.

Find out what to sell. You have to make sure that what you invest in will sell. You don't want to be the guy trying to sell magic mushrooms when everyone has "mollies" in their pocket. At the same time, you want to have a safe client base, so bath salts is probably not a great idea.

Get a connect. In order to sell something, you have to have something. This means you either have to grow/manufacture it yourself, or find someone who does.

Diversify your sources. Don't spend too much time and money on one connect. You want to have options because then your clients will have options.

This is also necessary to survive when product becomes scarce. When one source is dry, another may be flowing.

Attract customers. No point in having an inventory of drugs if you have no customers to sell them to. The amount of advertisement and customer increase depends on how risky you are willing to get. While most customers will come to you via word of mouth, you have to attract an initial amount of customers first.

Chapter Two:

Establishing Your Operation

In addition to acquiring inventory of product, you need to have a digital scale. Make sure this scale is a good one because you will be spending a decent amount of your life with it. If you ever need to make sure that your scale is on point, fold up a dollar bill and place it on the scale. One U.S. dollar bill weighs one gram. If it does not weigh one gram, then your scale is off and it may need recalibrating.

Most head shops or shops that sell marijuana smoking accessories can recalibrate your scale for you with weights. If they don't offer that in your area, or they just refuse to help, don't fret. You can go online and buy the weights to calibrate the scale yourself. Another thing you can do, is just take into account how much over or under your scale is, and adjust the amount of product accordingly.

If a dollar bill weighs .5 instead of 1.0, then know that when your product is weighing out to .5, you actually have one gram instead. If it reads .5, then you've weighed out a gram in actuality because your scale is .5 under. Tracking? It would be best to recalibrate your scale, but when you can't, this method works fine so long as you keep checking to see how much a dollar bill weighs on your busted ass scale.

Another thing you will need to purchase is baggies. I would say that you should just steal these from craft stores, but drug dealing is one thing, stealing is a whole other thing altogether. That aside, you still need baggies.

You can get whatever baggies you want, but make sure that they appear professional and don't say "Zip██" across the front. You want to advertise *your* business, not Zip██'s. Just because you're in a vice industry, it doesn't mean you cannot be a professional. Trust me on this, it will help you in the long run.

Most dealers get different sized baggies for many reasons. I used different sizes because it helped me on a subconscious level. You see, I would use the smallest baggie possible to fit whatever order came in. If someone wanted an eighth (3.5 grams, remember?), I would stuff it into a bag that would comfortably fit a dub (2.0 grams) only.

I did this because it gave the appearance of being abundant. When a customer looked at the bag, he or she would think, "Man, I just got a bunch of weed for only x amount of dollars!" You don't want customers to look at a dub in a bag that can hold a half ounce (14 grams). It looks pathetic. They will be thinking one of two things; either "Man, this big ass bag for a little tiny dub?" or "This dude probably did not give me what I paid for". Either way, you look like a jackass.

Sometimes, during holidays, it is nice to have festive bags. During Halloween, I used baggies that had jack-o-lanterns, and on Christmas, I used baggies with Christmas trees on them. Whether it helps to sell more product or not, I enjoyed it and so did my customers.

More importantly, you need a way for your customers to contact you, and you don't really want to use your personal cell phone. You should seriously consider getting a prepaid phone as soon as you can afford the extra expense. It helps with safety and secrecy should you be sought after on drug charges, and it also helps with expanding your business. More on this in chapter three.

You're also going to need to store all of those drugs you have. If you have weed, I suggest storing in mason jars to ensure freshness. You can also store your product in the refrigerator so that it doesn't lose its potency. If you're selling wax, which is a concentrated form of THC, the active chemical in marijuana, then you should definitely store it in the refrigerator. I recommend cutting a cotton swab in half, getting the cotton wet, and taping it to the lid of the mason jars that contain your herb. This keeps the weed from over drying and dropping in weight.

If you chose meth as your product line, you can rest assured knowing that it stores for years. Store your meth in a jar, or even some Tupperware, but a jar works best. Take a silica packet (can be found in packages of beef jerky and in some medicine bottles), and place it in your meth container. This will keep moisture from clumping it up if it's in powder form. It will also keep pieces from sticking together if it's in shard form.

So let's say you've gotten your product, gotten baggies, and you've gotten customers lined up. You have to decide how you are going to get it to them. There's the "delivery service method", the "come to me method", or a "public meeting spot method".

I would stay away from selling at home. A lot of lazy drug dealers, or drug dealers who don't care either way sell from home. This can lead to getting robbed, or getting busted. Besides, you don't want a bunch of people to know where you live, but if that's how you want to sell, you have to be smart about it.

Require *all* customers to stay for a minimum of 30 minutes. Anything less looks suspicious to prying eyes. When a customer comes over, greet them and let them in fast. Lead them to the transaction area, making sure that your money and product is hidden in a different location. **You do not want them to know where your money and product are located.**

After the transaction is complete, let them watch TV or offer them something to drink. Be hospitable. Often times, the customer will feel the need to share his recently purchased goods with you. At this point, you can take him up on one of the biggest perks of being a dealer, or tell him that he doesn't have to feel obligated to share with you.

Whatever you do, please make sure you are safe. Again, it goes without saying, but make sure you have a way to defend yourself against an attack. Use a gun, use a knife, use pepper spray, and make sure you always keep a close eye and ear on them. Most weed customers are friendly and very much laid back, but that doesn't mean you should take any chances.

The delivery service method is great because it offers two things; excellent customer service and it acts as the additional service required by California State Law for medical marijuana collectives. You see, in some medical marijuana states, the law requires that the person providing the medicine offers an additional service. Delivery is included in the law's recommendation.

With the delivery service, I would suggest having a minimum amount established. If the customer does not want to purchase at least a certain amount to make it worth your while, then what's the point of delivering it? Stick to certain areas and offer free delivery to those places so long as they purchase an eighth or more. If they want less, you can either charge a delivery fee to compensate for your travel, or decline their patronage all together.

This method is not entirely safe either, so some pitfalls to watch out for include robbery or getting pulled over. Make sure your car is working properly, including all of the lights and signals. Make sure your registration is up to date and you are driving like normal. This will decrease your chances of getting pulled over. This doesn't mean drive like a grandma. That just makes you look suspicious.

As far as getting robbed, you are really at the mercy of your customers. Obviously, some areas are safer than others but just in case, I would suggest carrying some type of weapon. This does not mean you should carry a gun. **Do not carry a gun**! I'm a firm believer in the Constitution of the United States of America, but for some reason having a drug *and* a gun charge is the worst thing imaginable. The court will have a witch hunt with you.

Instead, buy a "tire checker" from a truck stop. These tire checkers are obviously just billy clubs, but their name holds up if police want to harass you. Pepper spray is also legal to own in most places. You could also carry a straight razor sharp enough to cut someone's head clean off but because their main intention is for shaving, you can carry it around on you.

The good thing about running a delivery service is that most customers can appreciate that in a big way. People are lazy, and sometimes they are just plain tired. If you go to them, they are more inclined to repeat business. If a pizza joint didn't offer delivery, how much money do you think they would make? As far as customer service goes, delivery is the best.

The method that works in favor of the dealer is the public meeting place method. This can be anywhere you want it to be. Not only is it the safest route, but sometimes it's more convenient because you will inevitably get a call for some product while you are out shopping or at dinner. You can tell them to meet you there and it becomes convenient for you. With this method however, you cannot have a minimum amount rule. If they are coming to you, they get to choose how much they buy.

Regardless of your distribution method, you have to "be on point". This **means you cannot short**

someone. If they are buying an ounce (28 grams) then give them a full ounce. In all reality, you should make sure the bag is little heavy. If someone buys a gram, weigh out 1.2 grams or at the very least, 1.1 grams.

If they double check your sacks, which they will, they will see that you gave them more than they paid for and will undoubtedly appreciate that. This will garner you repeat business plus the massive likelihood that they will tell their friends about it, gaining you even more clients.

Furthermore, **charge accordingly**. If your product is not as good as you'd like for it to be, let your customers know and charge them fair prices for it. You better not try to sell someone low quality product at high quality prices, especially after reading this book. If you do, not only do you look like a dirt bag, but you will also lose a ton of business that you can never get back.

So, you have a client who needs a quarter ounce (7 grams). You've weighed it out to 7.2 grams, and you have chosen the delivery method. You immediately drive to their location because if you waste time, they will go elsewhere. No one likes "drug dealer time", where the dealer says ten minutes and shows up two hours later.

You show up to their place quickly and you are parked out front. Text or call them to let them know you have arrived. They will either tell you to come to the door or they will come out to your car. When you hand them the product, often times they do this weird handshake/handoff thing that can be rather confusing.

They will have the money in their hand, act like they are going to shake your hand, and then place the money in it instead. At the same time, you are expected to hand them the product. I don't like this transaction style but it happens. Despite being awkward, it makes for uncomfortable banter like, "How are ya, welp there ya go" or whatever.

I like to accept their money giving handshake first, and then hand them an envelope with the product stuffed inside. The envelope helps to conceal the contents from prying eyes and also gives you a second to count the money without appearing rude. While they peer inside the envelope, quickly check to see you have received the price you charged. California and its surrounding states typically charge about $60-$70 for a quarter ounce of weed.

Appearance is a very important part of being an illicit salesman, so it is equally important that we discuss it. According to the media, dealers are evil scum bags and subsequently must look like evil scum bags, right?

When you see a drug dealer on TV, he often appears to be male. He is also often "urban" or "ghetto". He prefers to wear a hoodie instead of a coat, and of course he drives an '80s model luxury sedan with rims bigger than his one bedroom apartment. This is not only incorrect, but it is offensive to illicit salesmen everywhere.

Do not be an idiot that wears a flat billed hat with the sticker still on it, or shirts that have the word *swag* screen printed on the front. Don't drive a car that stands out in any way. Not only does this make you look stupid, but it attracts unwanted attention.

Some of the most successful illicit salesmen dress like middle class conservatives; clean button up shirts, slacks, and shoes that don't require you to Velcro up the ankles. They keep their facial hair groomed, and their hair combed.

Cars you should think about driving do not include glowing lights underneath or "mad beats" in the trunk. Regular sedans, trucks, or minivans that are common in the area are a perfect vehicle for an illicit salesman. Make sure you keep that vehicle clean and neat, and that all lights are working properly.

If you don't have a day job, try to think of an excuse as to why you aren't seen leaving for work in the morning, or why you are almost always home yet still able to keep the power on. People will begin to ask, it is only a matter of time. You need to have a logical explanation ready.

With today's rapidly growing technology, it is more common to see people making a living working from home via the internet. It is not outlandish to tell someone you work from home. It does not matter what you tell them because unless they have it out for you, they are not going to look into it much further. Most Americans are too narcissistic to worry about your life in great detail.

You can tell them you are a freelance writer, or a blogger, or even a day trader. It would be best if you can educate yourself on a work from home job. Most people will believe whatever you say, so long as you maintain appearances. This is a major component of your new operation.

Another key component in this industry is **customer retention.** Without your customers, you are nothing. If you weren't around, they would just go to another dealer. If *the customer* wasn't around, you wouldn't have a business. It's important to keep those people happy.

Aside from making your sacks just a little bit heavy, you should also consider giving your loyal customers discounts every once in a while. One of the reasons to keep coming back to you is that you are a giving dealer. You should also let your loyal customers know when you have new product before you let others know.

The easiest way to let your customers know you have new product is to send them a simple text message. People like to know when you have new stuff, and often times are interested enough to ask for prices. You don't want them to go around looking for product, you *must* let them know what you have and when you have it.

Be mindful, however, that spam messaging is not conducive to your business. If you constantly text or call someone about buying some of your product, they will feel that you are badgering them. You know how you feel when a Jehovah's Witness knocks on your door? Yeah, that's what you are doing when you spam someone. One time text messaging is good, if they don't reply, assume they don't want any and move on.

Customer retention also depends on how you handle disputes. If someone claims you shorted them a gram or something along those line, immediately offer to make it right for them the next time they pick up from you.

One example is when I sold a guy a half ounce of good quality marijuana. It wasn't the best weed ever, but it was still pretty good stuff. After the transaction, I left the meeting spot and returned home. He sent me a text message claiming I had shorted him two grams, only giving him 12 grams.

I was surprised when I read the message because I pry myself on being a little heavy handed when it comes to weighing out sacks. Despite that, I offered to rectify the issue the next time he made a purchase from me. I didn't offer to fix it right then because of two reasons.

The first reason is that it would mean another trip. With gas prices comparable to an hourly wage entry level position, fuel has become a luxury. Wasting that fuel is a bad idea. The second reason is that I have just given him one more reason to buy from me again. In order to get his two grams, he has to make another purchase. This is called job security. Some guys lie when they say you shorted them, so you may as well make the most of a bad situation.

Pricing is something you will have to do one day at a time. Obviously, you will have to find out what other people are charging for the same thing, and go based off of that.

You may have heard, "never get high off your own supply". While I suggest that you don't try some of the harder stuff, like **meth** or **heroin**, it is vital in order to know how much to charge for weed. Meth and heroin sell themselves and people will buy it because they tend to become junkies. As far as weed goes, you have to smoke at least one bowl from every supply so you can know the flavor, the way it feels as you inhale, and the high you get from it, including but not limited to the duration of the high. If you don't, how can you know what to charge your clients?

If the stuff you've acquired is some of the best stuff you've tried, you can feel confident in knowing that your prices can be a little bit higher than other people, and it will still sell. However, if you do have some really amazing stuff at higher prices, make sure you have some lower grade product at lower prices. Here's an example of a conversation you will encounter, and how you should reply:

Customer: "What do you have, and what are the prices?"

You: "I have some Dutch Treat (strain), and it's top shelf. 15 a gram."

At this point, the customer will do one of three things; Agree to purchasing some at your price, ask for a lower price, or ignore you for the rest of your life. If they ignore you or ask for a lower price, here is how you should respond:

You: "If you're looking to save money, I have this other strain for 10 a gram. It's not as premium as that Dutch Treat, but it's still really good bud."

Instead of losing out on $15, you earn $10. While you may not have sold off your Dutch Treat, you did sell something. Save the "top shelf" stuff for when you get a connoisseur.

Let's review:

Acquire your supplies. It is not enough to have drugs. You have to be able to store those drugs, measure those drugs, and package those drugs. Giving someone some drugs in a melted cigarette wrapper is high school shit. This is the big show.

Choose a distribution method. You are the beacon that brings the customers and their drugs together. Use a multitude of the distribution methods to see what works best for you and your future goals as a salesman. Remember to watch out for the pitfalls of each method and have a plan to deal with them.

Customer retention. The most important part of your business is the customer, so don't forget it. Make your customers happy. If they are upset, fix it.

Get high on your own supply. This doesn't mean to consume all your profits. However, you *do* need to know what to charge for your stuff. Knowing how the high is can help you decide what to charge.

Appearance. This is the most valuable part of chapter two. You need to blend in. If you look like a drug dealer, walk like a drug dealer, talk like a drug dealer, then you must be an investment banker, said no one ever. There's a reason we have stereotypes. Think of yourself as a clandestine agent and that you have to keep your identity a mystery because your mission is top secret. It's kind of fun that way.

Chapter Three:

Growing Your Business

In any business, the entrepreneur wants to take his company to the next level. Honestly, it is best if you can hold off expansion for a while so that you can make your operation air tight. You are ready to move on if you have mastered all of the points from chapter two.

You expand by attracting more customers, so one trick many salesmen like to use is getting some referrals. In order to get referrals, you have to make an incentive for the person who is doing the referring.

Some people offer free drugs as an incentive. This is the preferred method, since its wholesale cost is much less than retail value, whereas the customer only sees the retail value. This makes it seem like you are giving them a lot, when in reality, it doesn't affect your bankroll at all. You end up saving money in the long run! When a user gets a free fix, they love you that much more and they will spend their "savings" with you in the future.

Tell your clients that if they refer their friends, they will get a little extra the next time they make a purchase from you. I usually gave .5 grams or one whole gram, but never more. The only time you want to give them more, is when someone they refer buys a large amount from you, but you're not there yet.

You can also offer discounts for referrals. Both your regular client and the referred client get a percentage off their next purchase. This makes them both start referring people to you, and then it's as if **you have a little marketing army working for you** without them even knowing it! You may think offering discounts is bad and loses money, but try telling that to Walm██.

If you are past this point, and your customers' demands are exceeding your man power, **it is time to take on a crew member**. Yes, you read that right. Just like in any other business, you will need to hire an employee. This has to be someone you trust, and someone who trusts you as well. If there is no trust, then assumptions will be made about who's cheating who and there can be a huge problem.

This person you trust, let's call him Rickey, is going to be working for you. You have to take care of him. If you don't, you will eventually get what you deserve. You will be "fronting" (giving an amount of drugs for free on credit) Rickey some drugs at a slightly marked up price, but not so high that there is no meat on the bone for him.

If an ounce of weed cost you $150, then front that ounce to Rickey for $200. That gives you an extra $50 profit without having to do *any* work whatsoever, and Rickey gets to rake in $80 for busting his ass for you. He won't mind that the mark up is higher than normal prices because he's getting it on a front, *and* he's making a bigger profit margin than you. This will make him happy, and you money.

When you do this, establish a day for Rickey to pay you what he owes and pick up more product from you. Thursday is typically a good day because he will be ready for the weekend's orders that start coming in on Friday around lunch time.

Another way you can start building your crew is by delegating shifts. This only works if your crew member lives in your area. Remember that prepaid phone? Much like a regular company, this is your business line. Let's say you desire working from 8am to 8pm, you can pass the phone off to Rickey at 8pm and officially be off duty! Now, all the calls and texts coming in are received by Rickey.

While you're dreaming about being the real Walter White (just a pussier version), Rickey is out selling your product. Come 8am, after you finish breakfast, Rickey hands the phone and the *money* off to you to continue the operation. Hold Rickey accountable, and make sure the money and the inventory is counted by the both of you at the end of each shift to ensure fairness.

A lot of dealers will advise aspiring entrepreneurs to avoid fronting anyone. They are afraid the person they fronted won't pay them back. This is a valid fear, and I will show you how to deal with that in the next chapter. For now, know that fronting a crew member is not only vital to growth, but it will make your life so much easier.

When you expand, you are giving yourself the option to take some time off. No one ever said hustling was easy. On the contrary, it was one of the most stressful, time consuming jobs I've ever had. You are always getting calls; day and night, holiday or not. **Money doesn't sleep**, **and there's no rest for the wicked**. Face it, you need to start building your crew.

Aside from gaining trustworthy employees, consider looking for other territories. If you are only selling to people in a four mile radius, consider getting your product into other communities. That's what "Donnie" did when he started hustling crystal meth.

Donnie was a privileged kid from an upper middle-class white family in a predominately upper middle-class white town. He made a lot of poor choices, and was addicted to meth by the time he was 14.

Knowing that he could not afford his habit, he needed to find a way to earn some cash. He lived across the street from the high school, so he was in some prime realty to make a killing.

He started hustling while he ditched class, and made a pretty good chunk of change. The money started flowing in! He was able to buy his own game consoles without having to wait until Christmas! He was able to buy his own clothes from high end stores, and he even bought himself an old classic car that was all fixed up!

Luckily, Donnie saw the potential and decided to kick that nasty habit. He saw it as a business opportunity, and knew he had to expand into different territories. He was going to build an empire...

He had a friend who lived in a different town, maybe ten miles away. Donnie and his friend had an agreement that every week the supply would be dropped off, and the revenue would be picked up.

He was fronting his friend some product, and his friend would then sell it off to customers in *that* town. This gave Donnie an advantage; he now distributes product in two different territories, one of which he doesn't even have to do the work.

You are going to want alliances when you expand. Other successful dealers in the area may hear about you, and they may want to purchase product from you as well. Offer them bulk, and keep your prices at rock bottom for them. You may not make as much as you would if you piece your product out on the street, but you do get to build rapport.

You want to do this because you can make money off of them while keeping them off of you. This is a peaceful way to take out the competition. No violence necessary, yet you still get the same effect! All of *their* clients are getting high off of *your* stuff!

Let's say they want to buy a pound of cocaine off of you. You bought that pound for $9,000, so mark it up very little. Offer it to them at $10,000, and expect to drop down to $9,500. Make them feel like they are getting a deal by giving them a deal. Now you have yourself a life customer who will purchase a large chunk of your inventory, thus reducing your overhead and your debt. While their business grows, so does yours! Remember, just because you're a "drug dealer" doesn't mean other dealers are your enemy.

There will come a time in your career that you will contemplate selling in bulk only. You may think it is best to buy 5 lbs. of weed, and sell it off by the QP. While you do sell off your inventory faster, there are a few things to consider when you sell in bulk.

Normally, selling in bulk sounds appealing, and there are many advantages to it. When you expand, it is normal to start selling in these larger amounts because you do less transactions. Less transactions means less opportunities to get caught, and more free time for yourself. These are big perks, which you can of course use to your advantage. But don't give up on the little guys.

When you sell to the regular, every day consumer whose typical purchase is no more than an eighth, you make a larger profit margin. By selling in bulk only, you lose out on that market. Wouldn't it be best to diversify and sell in both bulk *and* retail? If you want to sell in bulk only, that's OK. Maybe you were cut out for "brokering" in bulk.

In order to expand, you have to be able to keep supply flowing. That is why it was suggested earlier on to acquire multiple sources for your product. If you do go dry, you won't be able to provide your customers with what they need, and they will go elsewhere.

If they leave you and shop around, you will be forced to try and get them back, or get new customers. This puts you in a perpetual state of the "startup". You are constantly trying to find customers whose relationships are never built upon, leaving you in the beginner's circle.

If you find yourself dry and your customers leave you, don't panic. When you get new product, you can get your old clients back by offering discounts. While you may be losing money upfront, you are attracting your old clients back. Now, the next time they come around, you can charge regular price and recoup whatever you lost when you went dry.

Aside from gaining momentum in your own market, consider exporting your goods to other states. In California, weed is somewhat inexpensive. If I took an ounce that cost me $150, I could sell that ounce as is for $300 in almost any state that is not Washington, Oregon, or Colorado.

Consider sending some of your product to a friend or relative in a different state. I know that sounds dangerous and scary, and while it is a felony if you are caught, there are ways to ease your mind.

First, decide what carrier you are going to use. I used all three of the big ones, and that includes the United States Postal Service. It does not really matter what carrier you use because they all use the same methods when transporting packages.

Before you ship out your weed, have your recipient set up a P.O. Box, or use a vacant house as the address. The latter option is a little more time consuming on package day, but at least it is safe. We will discuss this in greater detail in another paragraph.

The P.O. Box you want the recipient to set up is not the one at the actual post office. If he or she goes to the one at the actual post office, he or she will have to give them personal information and to top it all off, they have cameras all over the place. Instant felony, just add carelessness.

Have them set up a P.O. Box at another facility that is not a government building. There are civilian store fronts that offer packaging, shipping, and even sell stationary. These are the guys you want to go to. A lot of them are owned and operated by locals, which means that you are not only supporting the local economy (as any dealer should because they, too, are local), but you are also able to build a relationship with the people working there. It's good to be on someone's friend list, especially if something bad were to happen.

Now, the safer alternative is to have it shipped to an empty house that no one lives in. Be careful not to have it sent to a house that was vacant, and is now occupied. Your recipient will have to stay on top of that.

Make sure that when you send it out, you **do not require a signature**. You just want them to drop it at the door, and leave. Your recipient will be waiting patiently out of sight for the package. When the carrier drops it off and leaves, the recipient should very hastily, acquire the package, and leave.

This method helps to prevent busts, because if the police are sent to the empty house, they will only find the package. Your recipient will just sit quietly from a distance, watching. Now they double as a spy for you, and can tell you when the jig is up. Now you know to lay low for a while and on top of that, your recipient dodged a bullet as well. This is the safest method.

Things you are going to need:

1. **Rubber Gloves**

2. **Large Candle**

3. **Sealing bags (vacuum sealed works best, but expensive)**

4. **Drill**

5.　　Lighter

Before you ship, you will need to seal your product up. While there is no tricking the drug sniffing dogs by masking scent, there is a way to delay the release of the scent. Dogs can smell through layers. For example, when you smell lasagna, you just smell lasagna. When a dog smells lasagna, it smells the noodles, it smells the cheese, it smells the sauce, it smells the meat, it smells the seasoning, it smells everything individually. You cannot mask the scent with stronger scents. If anything, it makes you look more suspicious to the people loading and unloading packages. You have to delay the scent.

First, wash your hands very well. Put on rubber gloves, and **do not touch the drugs**. If you do touch the drugs, don't touch anything else. Throw the gloves away, wash your hands again, and put on new gloves. It is imperative that you do not let the drugs, and the shipping materials touch!

Take a large candle, and cut the bottom off. Let's call this part you just cut off "the cap". Take your drill, the bit size doesn't matter, and drill a hole in the bottom of the remaining candle (not the cap, the candle). Your goal is to hollow out the candle, while leaving about an inch of solid candle at the top. Do not drill all the way through the candle. Use the drill to widen the hole you made. The wax is soft, so don't apply too much force. The candle should be able to perform the same function as a drinking glass if you turned it upside down.

Now, take your product, and place it inside a sealing bag. Take your gloves off, and throw them away. Wash the bag and your hands, making sure there is no residue on the outside of the bag. Put on another pair of gloves, and stuff the bagged up product into another bag. Repeat the washing process. I know this seems redundant, but trust me, better safe than sorry!

Now, once you have the product double bagged and clean, place it inside the hollowed out candle. Take the cap, and melt it back on to the candle to make it one whole piece again. Make sure you seal all the way around the seam with the melted wax. Let the candle cool completely for about 45 minutes to an hour.

Put on new gloves, and place the candle inside another two bags. Now your product is ready to go inside the box. Eventually, the smell will come out over time. If you can't smell it, it doesn't mean the dogs can't, so you shouldn't do this part until you are ready to ship the package out.

Make sure you are not shipping the product in a used box. Get a new box, new tape, and package it all up nice and neat. If it looks sloppy, it attracts attention. I know this sounds stupid, but according to Kevin, an employee of mine who works in logistics at a reputable shipping company, they look for packages that may seem "out of place" or "lazily put together".

When you go to ship, make sure you did not allow for even the slightest possibility of drugs coming into contact with the outside of the package. This is the most important part! Even if the box sat in your passenger seat, if you have ever had drugs there, chances are you now have residue on the outside of your package strong enough for the dogs to pick up.

As you fill out your shipping form, make sure you do not require a signature on the receiving end. That defeats the purpose of the P.O. Box and the vacant house plan. You will also have to claim what is inside, so just say something no one will want to steal, and customs will have no interest in. If you say it is edible, then customs *will* open the package. Make sure whatever you claim weighs about the same as what you are sending out. Don't worry about placing insurance on the package. If it gets lost, chances are it got found, but not by friendlies.

Do not overnight the package! One of the biggest mistakes aspiring exporters do is overnight their product, thinking it will not have time to be searched by authorities. You are wrong. When you overnight a package, it gets put on a plane, and everything going on that plane gets checked by drug dogs and x rays. Keep a low profile, and mail it out at the lowest priority. While it may get placed on a plane at some point in time, the threat level of your package being a terrorist's bomb is significantly dropped. No terrorist would take their time getting a bomb on to a plane. Keep the priority low, and no one will look twice.

Let's Recap:

Attract new customers. Do this by being social, and honest. Give people what they want and they will always come back.

Get a crew member. While some people suggest that you never front product, sometimes it is necessary to grow. Besides, think of all the free time you'll have by having someone *else* sell your drugs!

Expand into other markets. It pays to make friends who are already dealing. You can get your product to them and they will sell it off. While your profit margin is not as big as when you sell it yourself, in order to grow you have to expand your market.

Try exporting. Drugs are being shipped all over the world, it might be wise to tap into that market.

Chapter Four:

When Push Comes to Shove

It sucks, I know. No one ever *wants* to see this side of the business, but sometimes it is a necessary evil. **There will be a time when you get burned**, it happens to everyone. But what do you do when it happens? How do you recoup? **What is going too far?** All of these questions will be answered in this chapter.

Before you learn about how to respond with force, you should try to take as many preventative measures you can. For example, when you front Rickey, you make sure you know where he lives. Make him aware that you know.

Also, whatever money you make off of him, place 50% away somewhere. Think of this as insurance. If he makes you a total of $4,000 this week, put $2,000 away in your secret insurance stash. Then, if a pound gets robbed from him or he steals it himself, you already have the $2,000 to cover the costs of it stashed away.

If for some reason, you need to fight fire with fire, there are many ways you can do it. You are only limited by your imagination. If situations get worse, you may want to consider hiring outside help. But first, try to prevent the problems before they arise.

Hopefully you can avoid simple mistakes by simply creating a set of rules, and abiding by them strictly. One of those rules should be **never front a customer.**

This is the worst thing you can do. It's not only likely that the customer will never pay you back, but worse, they will think they can get fronts from you all the time. This will cause them to rack up a huge debt they will never repay, and you just got some sleaze ball high for free.

Ron was a customer I had for about a three month span. He bought half ounces from me at $100 once a week. One day, after unsuccessfully trying to negotiate deals with me, he agreed to meet up for another transaction.

I met Ron, who promptly jumped into my car, and handed me a stack of fives and ones wrapped up in a 20 (this is something a lot of customers do to hide the fact that they're paying you in small bills and they hope you don't get upset).

He told me that he only had $90, and that he could give me the rest the next time he picks up. Being a nice guy, I allowed him to have the remainder that he owed on credit. You know what happened? I never saw Ron again. He never answered my calls, my texts, and he of course never tried to buy from me again.

What I should have done was tell him to get out, and call me back when he has the full amount, or offer to give him less. Under no circumstances should you front a customer product. Sure, it was only 10 bucks, but it's the principle. **This isn't a charity, it's a business**.

If for some reason you are forced to make a threat, you cannot back down. Don't say you are going to kill someone unless you are actually going to do it. That makes you look weak. Always keep your word and never back down, although, I would highly advise against murder.

Martin was another dealer in my area, who was black and worked the black customers. I wanted to tap into that market, but black people tend to only trust other black people, and I don't blame them. In order to get into that market, I had to sell to Martin.

I came to him with the proposition that I would front him some product. I knew Martin pretty well as we worked together at a previous job, and he was always trustworthy there. The deal was pretty simple; I would give him a QP (quarter pound), and he would pay me $700 after he sold it.

The plan worked pretty well, I was selling my product to the black community without putting in the footwork. Life was pretty good, at least until Martin decided to hire on a crew member.

Every day, after Martin and his crew member closed up shop, they would stash the earnings away in a jar. When the jar would get full, they would count out the cash, and see what was mine, and what was theirs.

Well, the crew member got in to some money troubles and really needed to pay his bills. Knowing he still had product to make some money on, he decided to dip into the jar. He was using *my* money to pay *his* bills, hoping to earn it all back with the remainder of product.

Normally, I would understand. I'm a reasonable guy, and I have been known to pay for people's medical marijuana cards, and gas, and even legal fees. If he would have come to me, I would have helped him pay his bills. But he didn't.

A week went by, and I didn't hear from Martin, so I called him up. He told me what had happened, and that he was trying to resolve the problem. I'm no micro-manager, so I gave him three weeks to fix the problem and come up with the $700 they both owed me. This was more than reasonable. Time went on, and no money came in. I was pissed!

I sent an employee of mine, Jesse, over to his neighborhood. Jesse was notorious for being a little crazy. Actually, for being *really* crazy. Let's just say I've been in Jesse's cross hairs before, and while I may have survived, others aren't as lucky.

Jesse watched this neighborhood for a while, and when the moment was right, he approached Martin's house. He knocked on the door and Martin answered, unknowingly. Jesse introduced himself and asked if Martin's car was for sale, to which Martin replied, "No, I don't plan on selling it." Jesse told him, "You might have to, to pay [673126] back." This might not appear so scary, except for the fact that we had no idea where he lived, so he knew that if I could find his home, I could do a lot worse if necessary.

Martin grew nervous, and tried to talk his way out. I give him credit for keeping his cool, though. A lot of guys can't do that. "Look, I already talked to [673126], we worked it all out," Martin told him. Jesse only said, "If you don't pay up by Monday, I'll be back, and I'll shoot this whole fucking place up."

Needless to say, Martin paid me the full $700, plus an additional $100 for waiting so long for it. I gave him the $100 back because like I said, I'm a reasonable guy. Luckily, I didn't have to sic Jesse on him, but if he hadn't paid, Jesse would've done to him what he has done to other people who like to lie, cheat and steal. In most cases, you won't have to push the issue too far, but in that off chance you do, you can't back down.

Sometimes, you will come across a shit talking type dealer who is your competition. These guys are all the same. They have very tiny penises, parents who don't love them, and have never had a meaningful relationship with a woman. These guys are turds.

This fellow named Hector started selling his product in my area. He actually got me in to the business by piquing my interest, so I let him sell his stuff without trying to hustle in on him. Until he got stupid with me.

He would come see me with product that was actually pretty good stuff. A lot of people liked it, hell, I liked it. I decided it was time to make this guy an ally instead of competing with him. After all, I *want* to be able to get my hands on popular strains, and Hector had a good connect!

He came to me, boasting about how amazing his stuff is, so I offered to buy it off him. He agreed, but wanted to charge me full retail price, all the way up to the half-pound. I couldn't let him screw me like that, so I only bought an eighth to try out, and to give out as samples to help build up the market for it. He charged me $40 for that eighth, but whatever, this was a small investment so I didn't mind paying a little tax on it.

Later, he left, and I thought the sack looked a little light, so I weighed it. It weighed out to only 2.5 grams, which is one gram shy of an eighth. Not only did he over charge me, but he skimped on weight! What a greasy worm!

I kept my mouth shut, and talked with him about purchasing a large amount. Just like in chapter one, I staged it so that I could meet with the grower. I purchased a huge amount from the grower, and I also told him to watch out for Hector because I saw him get arrested on a deal. I said that the cops had him for intent to distribute, and to be careful because Hector has been known to rat for other things.

I don't know if Hector would rat or not, but judging by the way he looked with his ghetto clothing, self-tinting eyeglasses, and supped up '90s model Lumina, he had stool pigeon stamped all over his face.

Hector was never able to purchase from that grower again, and all it took was a little bit of doubt in the grower's mind. All I had to do was plant a little seed, and the grower did what he does best; he grew a giant, bushy plant with constant focus and attention. Hector asked me the other day if he could buy a $20 sack from me because now that's all he can afford to buy.

If for some reason, your business plans get crushed because of another person in the industry, it is time to **crush *them***. When someone messes with your business, they mess with your money, which messes with your livelihood. Don't feel bad about destroying someone else's livelihood.

One thing you should avoid is girlfriends or boyfriends, yours or anyone else's. A scorned lover can become your biggest enemy in a matter of minutes. This typically happens with women, but no matter their sex, a scorned lover often tries to get you caught.

Roger was a cool guy. He lived in the mountains, he liked my weed, and he had this cool philosophy on life about how the government is a bunch of tyrants and no one likes to mind their own business. I liked Roger.

We hatched a plan since he had a large lot, and I was looking to grow. I spent so much money setting up a grow operation on Roger's farm, and I even had a crew to do all the work in setting up, growing, harvesting, and even distributing it. It was like my own little franchise, and damn was I excited!

Roger slowly started to scare me a little bit with his conspiracy theories. I mean, I've been known to accept some conspiracy theories as possible truth, but this guy was going crazy! He was accusing Catholics and Jesuits and Freemasons of controlling the world, and the Jews were the foot soldiers, and yada, yada, yada. I was questioning my business with him.

One day, Roger got into it with his crazy girlfriend, and he kicked her out. Roger never told me, and then one day he called me up freaking out. "Dude, you gotta get up here and grab all your shit!" he exclaimed.

"What the fuck, Roger, what's going on?" I asked. I was completely confused!

He proceeded to tell me that his girlfriend went to the cops, and that she came up with a few officers to point out the grow sites. Roger told me that the Sheriff's Department was doing flybys earlier in the afternoon, and that they will be back.

I panicked, because I'm human too, and I flew up to the farm to grab all my plants. I lost out on all the equipment because I didn't have the logistics at the time. Luckily, the cops never busted *me* because I was in and out, but because it was late in the season, I was never able to recoup that loss. I was pissed. I stopped talking to Roger, telling him our business together is done. He lost his temper, and let his mouth write a few checks that his ass couldn't cash.

I decided later that I would get my money back somehow, and I devised a plan. You may have to do this someday as well, but know that you can avoid it if you stay away from people with wives/girlfriends/pussy boyfriends. I told Jesse about the farm, and how Roger moved his plants back out there, and that they were flowering up with some decent quality buds.

We waited until it was getting close to harvest, and we drove up to the old site. Roger had some dogs on the property I knew about, so we brought steaks and peanut butter. I covered the steaks in peanut butter, and tossed them over the fence to the dogs. They loved that shit! The meat made them happy, and the peanut butter kept their tongues busy so they couldn't bark.

We hopped the fence, and snuck over to each plot, chopping the plants at the roots. My heart was pounding! I could hear noises in the distance, and every time I did, I assumed it was Roger coming with his barbed wire baseball bat to catch me. I knew that I had to be cautious, but not paranoid. I snapped out of my funk, and got busy moving a little faster.

An hour later we had a van full of fresh, sticky herb. I was able to get my money back and then some. I don't know what happened to Roger, but I bet he's pretty upset about it still. You may have to do the same thing, too.

For a few years, I ran a transportation ring for all forms of drugs. Weed, meth, coke, and even all the cash from the transactions. It was a smooth operation, which you will learn more information on later, until I hired Leo.

Leo was a pretty cool guy for the most part. We had worked together at a retail job I once had back in the late '90s. It was a bullshit job that made me want to be a drug dealer in the first place.

Leo needed some extra money, and I knew he was on the level. What I didn't know, was that he was an alcoholic. That really threw a wrench in it for me.

I had a job running about 30 kilos of meth from Fresno to Portland twice a month. It was great income, but I needed to bring on another driver just in case one of us got busted, the other could get away with at least half of the product.

The convoy was all prepped, and the cars were loaded down. All we needed was Leo to show up. When he did, he was as drunk as he could be. The man drank himself retarded. How on Earth could he drive to Portland without crashing, or attracting attention? We had to teach him a lesson.

The boys took him out back, and we all circled him. He knew what was coming, even if he was completely hammered. We administered some Bostonian Justice; literally beating the shit out of him. We didn't kill him, or do permanent damage, because we're not ruthless, but we did teach him a valuable lesson. You know what else? He gave up drinking and has been sober for three years!

So, while it may suck to have to get your hands dirty, at some point you are going to out of necessity. Keep in mind that every experience can be a good one, but you have to have the right mindset. If you go into this with violence and hate and negativity on your mind, that's all you'll get out of it.

Recap time:

Take preventative measures. Don't set yourself up for failure, because more often than not, you are your own worst enemy.

Never front a customer. While customers are your life force in any business, don't play any bullshit games with them. If they want a front, tell them to get it from someone else. Business, not charity!

If you make a threat, make sure you can commit to it. If you're flaky on your threats, no one will take you seriously. Don't try to be Billy Bad Ass if you can't step up to the plate.

Contract out your dirty work. If you don't want to do the hardest part of this job, there are plenty of unemployed Americans out there who really need some money. Hire these hungry people! Just make sure they're on the level.

Hell hath no fury like a woman's scorn. Or any lover, for that matter. Try to avoid doing business with someone who is in a relationship. Chances are they will fight, and that heartbroken snitch will tell the police. Stay away.

Make competition your ally. If you can't, use your imagination to destroy them.

Teach the screw ups a lesson. Sometimes, you have to teach your employees a lesson. If they cross you, or mess up, don't be afraid to teach them that they are wrong.

Follow these tips, and it won't be long before you're the most respected dealer in town!

Chapter Five:

Transporting and Distribution

At some point, your network will find a way for you to seize a really good opportunity. This opportunity comes in many different forms, but one opportunity in particular is the sweet, sweet gig of transporting and the distribution of drugs. It is the most thrilling, and most rewarding job in the business.

When you transport product, the product is usually not yours, and therefore you have no real stake in the business. Your only job is to get it from Point A to Point B. You have no overhead, no customer service duties, and no real investment other than time. That time can vary from just a few hours in a car, to life without parole.

This is why it is so thrilling. The idea of having a car loaded up with some really illegal stuff, and sharing the road with highway patrol is like swimming with sharks on your period. Unless you're in the military, you will probably never experience adrenaline that intense. And that drug is free!

If you can't handle that much anxiety, then I suggest you don't find out what it is you are actually transporting. You can tell your client (or your hook up, whoever presented this job to you) that you do NOT want to know what you're transporting. This doesn't make it any more legal, but it will put your mind at ease because you won't be saying to yourself over and over, "I have a trunk full of cocaine, I have a trunk full of cocaine." Instead you will just be saying, "I have a trunk full of something. It could be drugs. It could be dead hookers. It could be kittens and puppies. I don't know, so I'll just listen to this static on the radio." You could do that, if you want to be a pussy about it.

I got my first start at transporting product when my connect asked me if I could drive 35 pounds of weed to L.A. from Hollister. He made it sound awesome! He said he would pay me $200 a pound, plus all my gas, my hotels, and even strippers if I wanted them. So of course I said yes, and I loaded up my car that night.

I drove non-stop until I hit Bakersfield, and I got a hotel. I parked my car within sight of my hotel room window because I had to leave the product in the car. It wasn't stuffed in duffel bags; my connect lined the trunk, and door panels with weed. Yeah, drug dogs would smell it, but at least there wouldn't be a duffel bag for the cops to look through if they tried to pull me over for some made up bullshit.

That night, after I checked in, I kept peering out at the car, making sure it was safe. I was anxious and stressed out about the safe keeping of that product. But then I realized, it wasn't my product! Yeah, I was in charge of delivering it to someone, but it wasn't mine to stress about. If something happens to it, and I did my part without making stupid choices, then it wouldn't be my fault! I was finally able to relax.

I brought a personal stash to smoke in the room. It was a non-smoking room, but isn't it obvious how I feel about rules and laws? I watched some TV, and just melted into the lumpy bed.

Right as I was about to pass out, I noticed some flashing lights, seeping through my window. Blue and red lights, flickering just outside. I nearly shit my pants. I flew out of bed, and almost dove out the window to see!

There they were; two cop cars, their lights on, and the officers standing there right behind my car. One of them had a canine on the leash, while the other had his weapon in hand. I was dead, I had to get the fuck out of there!

I rushed to the bathroom to see if I could fit through the window. I ripped the shower curtain open and looked. "What fucking window?" I asked myself. There wasn't one! I was proper fucked now, and I started sobering up.

I looked out the window again, this time I saw the dog barking at the back of my car. I'm sure you can imagine what was going through my head at this point. What could I do? Nothing, that's what. Time to face the music, the jig is up! It was a good run, but I knew this day would come eventually.

Suddenly, I see the cop rip a man away from between my car, and another car. There was a person hiding under my car that they were trying to arrest! I felt so relieved! They weren't suspicious of my car, or looking for me, they were trying to arrest some black kid that was hiding *under* my car. What a bullet I dodged!

My heart was racing, my adrenaline was skyrocketing, and my euphoria was increased ten-fold. This was the thrill I was talking about! From then on, I fell in love with transportation and distribution! Nonetheless, I had to get a good night's sleep because the next morning it was off to L.A.

I drove on, and at one point I was in front of a highway patrol officer for about 10 miles. That had my heart pumping for a while! Then I read a sign on the side of the freeway that said, "drug checkpoint ahead". I panicked at first, but then I realized what was really going on.

In the United States, **there is no such thing as a drug checkpoint.** Let that sink in for a minute. The whole design is entirely unconstitutional, and is therefore not allowed by any law enforcement (even though DUI/DWI checkpoints are completely unconstitutional, too).

You see, these dumb ass cops put up a sign that says "drug checkpoint ahead" in order to see who gets off the freeway. The person making a hasty exit is obviously carrying drugs, and then they can pull him or her over for whatever made up reason they deem fit.

After they pull that poor soul over, they pretend like they need to search the car. They get drug dogs, and they even force the drug dogs to give a "false alert". A false alert is when they make it appear that the dog is alerting to something, but they are actually being commanded to alert. This gives the cops the right to search your car, and the next thing you know, you're calling Saul to come represent you in court.

Do not try to dodge checkpoints of any kind. This gives you away. Instead, you have to just face the music, as they say. If it's your time to get busted, get a straw and suck it the fuck up. Keep on cruising through that checkpoint (remember, there is no such thing as a drug checkpoint, it's all a trick). You'll even feel like a real bad ass when you get through the close calls, so just stick it out.

When I arrived at my destination, I checked in with the "mark" or whatever you wish to call this middle class, white hippie with dread locks. He treated me like a welcomed visitor in his place by offering me food and drinks, and women. This whole time, I got to party in his home while he unloaded the product, and reassembled my car *perfectly.* No kidding, it was in better shape *after* he did his thing, like he went in and fixed shit that was wrong with my car.

After the good times rolled on, he gave me a small grocery bag filled with bundles of that other amazing green stuff; cash. I felt like Johnny Depp in that cocaine movie I can't name because of copyright infringement. I was on my merry way, $7,000 richer. It only took me one day of driving, and one day of partying.

Do you see the perks of this side of the business? It's exactly like being a really well paid employee. And the cash is quick, you don't have to actually close any sales! The sales are already made, you're just the delivery boy! I had to keep this gravy train rolling.

I decided to set up my own little ring of transporters. I had that little problem with Leo, but business was booming nonetheless. One of the higher level cartel guys had a manufacturing plant in Fresno. Well, technically it was just a few houses on the same street, but he was manufacturing just the same.

His guys would cook up some of the cheapest meth they could concoct, and ship it off to Oregon, where the market was young, and booming. I had the opportunity to get in on the ground floor; someone had to transport all that meth up north.

At first, it's just going to be you. No one else will be driving with you, unless you're a small part of a much bigger picture, and you are hired as one of many drivers. As far as your own operation goes, it's just going to be you for a long time.

Get ready for a life of crazy, heart pounding bullshit. It's a scary ride, especially when you are alone. A few tips to keep you safe can go a long way in survival here. Heed my warnings, and **take everything to heart.**

Your appearance is key here. Get yourself a decent car that doesn't have any problems. A shitty car can leave you dead in the water, and what happens if a Good Samaritan comes along to help you out? You're going to have to kill that poor bastard to keep your secret safe. Don't drive a lemon.

Take the time to make sure all of your lights are functioning. If for any reason they aren't, get them working as soon as possible, even if it means going bankrupt just to purchase a bulb. Any price is better than serving a sentence in a cage.

Now that your car is taken care of, maintained, and **clean** (yeah, clean that rust bucket inside and out, don't be a dirtbag), you can focus on *your* appearance. Think about what a drug dealer looks like. Picture that person's face, their clothing, picture the length of their hair. I'm guessing you either imagined someone dark skinned that wears baggy clothing and borderline female sunglasses, or Jesus. Bullshit, tell me I'm wrong. Get those images out of your head. We already talked a little bit about this!

They say never to judge a book by its cover. If you've read my other book, *How to Make Money in Your Spare Time*, then ask yourself why you bought it. Because of the cover! A book about making money with a guy wearing a ski mask on the cover seems like a solid investment, right? If there was a picture of a man washing cars, or saving pennies, you would not have bought it. It's the sad truth, but people are always judging books by their covers. People are always judging other people based on their appearances.

If you are a male, I would highly suggest that you keep your hair short, and clean cut. Always have a fresh shaved face, and if you can wear regular eyeglasses, even better. I suggest nice button up shirts, slacks, and dressier shoes. The higher class you present yourself, the less likely it is that you will be harassed by the police.

If you need to have some company while you transport the product, don't take a car full of dudes. Especially if they look like bums! I would recommend you take a woman of similar age, or no one at all. Even two men driving along on the freeway can be suspect enough to assume you are carrying drugs and money.

If you are a female, I suggest you have regular, natural looking hair and no facial piercings. Business casual looks really good because it gives everyone the impression you are a woman of importance and you have some big shot business shit to do. No one messes with a woman who appears powerful. That's a great weapon for your arsenal!

If you want to have company as a female, a car full of girls works for some reason. Just be advised that you may be sexually harassed at gas stations, or even by the police if they're feeling particularly confident in themselves. Chances are they will always let you off the hook though, so I wouldn't worry too much about coppers.

If you are having trouble trying to get your appearance down, I would recommend you study your surroundings. You obviously don't want to stand out, so try to fit in with others around you. If other people (who aren't harassed by law enforcement) dress in a certain way, try to follow suit. Being different, or individual makes you stick out like a giant rainbow colored dick at a country club. Don't attract attention to yourself!

If you are driving your product on the freeway, there are some rules to consider. Cops tend to be jerks about things. Let's face it, their job sucks and your job is awesome. They're jealous that they have to constantly do paperwork, sit in a stuffy car with no leg room, and face threats on a daily basis. How do they cope with that stress? They take it out on potential "perps". Now that you know what their mindset is, you can understand how to deal with them, but that is another chapter. First, you need to learn how to avoid them.

Freeways are the lifeline that keeps the heart of any country pumping with the blood of capitalism. Navigating this lifeline is important to any smuggler worth his weight in drugs. You must *always* obey the traffic signs, particularly the speed limit signs. If the speed limit is 65, you better be doing 65. Don't stress out about it, there is *some* leeway in speed limits, but I would never push it.

Avoid using the far left lane. Most people have come to believe that that lane is for people who are driving faster than the general population. Well, it's not! It is a passing lane, and while in most cases you won't be bothered for chugging along in the left lane, don't attempt it with drugs. Cops have been using this trick to pull people over for some time now. It works like this:

- The cop sees you, and you look kind of suspicious.
- They think to themselves, "this job is boring, what if I can bring down a drug smuggler today? Then my wife will have sex with *me* instead of that cool drug dealing college student across the street."
- They see you get into the fast lane and continue to drive, not using it as a passing lane.

- Now they have you right where they want you. They decide to get behind you, and light it up.
- You pull over, and they ask to look inside your car.
- You tell them no, so the drug dogs come.
- Now you're proper fucked!

Don't be tempted to use the "fast lane". It's a fast lane alright, a fast lane to your jail cell.

Another thing to consider is your driving etiquette. Let people go around you if you're driving too slowly for them. Let those fuckers get the ticket and save you from putting your house up as collateral for your bail bond.

Always use your turn signals. It should go without saying, but I know how you think already. You get excited, and you feel all pumped up from your newfound career, and you think you're a badass who doesn't use turn signals. Turn signals are for middle aged women, and old people who always forget that they're on. Wrong. Turn signals are for people who want to avoid getting pulled over.

A weird thing you might not think about now, is whether or not you need snow chains. I always bring them with me, except in the summer of course. But you never know when you have to drive through an area that gets snow. A lot of police in these areas love to catch people without snow chains. It's easy money for their department, but it can cost you a lot more than a ridiculously overpriced fine.

One time I was driving through to Nevada and hit Tehachapi. I needed snow chains there, and it was the law. I was prepared of course, so I made sure there was **no product in the trunk**, and I placed my tire chains ever so gently in the center. I'm glad I did, because this cop decided to pull me over, thinking I didn't have set of chains, and he could earn some funding for the department. When I popped my trunk, there they were. He was disgruntled about it, but he had to let me drive away. I felt like a champ; he felt like a chump!

It's not just about avoiding arrest, however. Snow chains are a necessity for safety if it snows. Just because you pay no regard to the law, it doesn't mean you should pay no regard to life.

At some point, you're going to be making some pretty decent money. You would be wise to reinvest it into your operation. Something other transporters do is "clone" a vehicle. These people have made enough money to afford this, and the more elaborate, the more expensive.

By cloning a vehicle, you are simply replicating it. You don't replicate regular cars and trucks, the idea is that you replicate commercial delivery trucks, city and county vehicles, even school busses. It has to be spot on, or you will get caught. One truck was stopped that had "Border Patron" stamped on it. Don't be retarded like that guy.

You start by deciding which type of vehicle you are going to replicate. Keep in mind, the bigger the vehicle and the more detailed the design, the more expensive it is going to be. I would recommend a parcel service truck or a phone/cable company truck, because:

A. You won't need an exempt license plate
B. No endorsements are required because there are no hazmat placards
C. Their decals and paint jobs are pretty easy to replicate

If you want to take on the challenge of cloning a county vehicle, keep in mind that you will need to acquire exempt license plates in some areas. This can be tricky, especially if you steal the plate, because that's going to get reported. You will have to fabricate one, and that can be expensive.

Some transporters have cloned police cars as their smuggling vehicle. This is ironic, and funny. Who runs a cop's license plate? Just remember, if you go this route and you are caught, you not only face drug charges, but now you face charges for impersonating a police officer as well; something you really should think about before trying.

Once you come into even more money, you can clone a shipping truck for a popular chain of low priced retail stores. Yes, we're talking semi-truck, big rigs with full sized trailers swaying behind them. Pay attention to all of the decals, though. You don't want anything to look odd.

Recap time!

Do not try to dodge checkpoints. This is obvious, and is a guaranteed one way ticket to prison. Roll the dice! How can you win the game if you don't play?

Appearance is key to survival. Don't look like a drug smuggler. Try to blend in, you and your car.

Avoid the fast lane. It is the fast lane to Jailtown. Don't use it. Cops use the excuse that it is actually a "passing lane", and therefore have given themselves the right to pull you over.

Use your driving etiquette. That means turn signals, headlights, no flashing of your high beams, unless you're a female and your nipples are hard. You can mail the pictures to me in prison at:

Have snow chains, and use other police avoidance measures. Just try your best to stay away from the law. Use snow chains to avoid tickets in winter. Make sure your car isn't a hazard to be on the road! It's not just about avoiding being caught, it's about saving lives, too!

Consider cloning a vehicle. It is expensive, but very cost effective. It's worth the money if you have it.

Chapter Six:

Dealing With Police and Arrest

Dealing with police is no cake walk. Lately, it seems like every day you hear some horror story of how police are dealing with the people they are sworn to protect and serve. Let's face it, they no longer protect and serve. Not all cops are bad, but most have an insane power trip. You will need to know how to navigate this minefield.

If you want to avoid police brutality, you need to know the law. Nothing gets a pig off your ass like knowing your rights! I would suggest you read up on the Constitution (if you live in the U.S.). Now, some local laws may prohibit something that is guaranteed in the Constitution. For example, in the U.S., a citizen is allowed to bear arms (have a gun). However, in some cities, guns may not be allowed. This of course infringes on your Constitutional Right, and if you wanted to push the subject matter in court, it is likely you will win. You want to avoid this altogether, so read up on all your laws; local or otherwise.

Two very important rights every U.S. Citizen is afforded is granted in Amendments IV and V in the Constitution (**Honorable Mention:** Amendment I for the sake of this book). These two Amendments grant you the right to protect yourself from the biased police state we currently reside in. Amendment IV protects you from warrantless searches, and Amendment V protects you from incriminating yourself. Here is Amendment IV:

Amendment IV

The right of the people to be secure in their persons, houses, papers and effects, against unreasonable searches and seizures, shall not be violated, and no Warrants shall issue, but upon probable cause, supported by Oath or affirmation, and particularly describing the place to be searched, and the persons or things to be seized.

What does this mean? Well, this says that no officer of the law can just search you, your car, or your home without a warrant. This warrant is an official document issued by a judge that will allow for the police to search your property legally. If a cop ever asks to search you, or your property, ask that motherfucker for a warrant. Be cautious, because cops are very tricky.

Often times, the cop will try to play the cool guy role. He will tell you that your only chance of avoiding arrest is by letting him check out what he wants. This is a lie, because you and I both know what it is you're hiding, and you are guaranteed to get arrested if he searches your belongings.

Cops are liars, believe it or not. They will do what it takes to get your ass arrested. They will tell you that you have no choice, that there is nothing you can do, but know that this is bullshit and these guys are just out looking for "action". The only time you should worry, is if you are driving.

When you are driving, the cop has a right to ask for your ID, and you have to show him it. Don't argue about the ID at this point. If you are on foot, you don't even have to talk to the cops. On foot, you are the king.

When cops harass you on foot, it should go like this:

You're walking along, you've got your backpack full of pre-bagged goods, and you're out to earn some cash. Suddenly, a squad car pulls up next to you, and an officer gets out. He asks what you're doing, and you can tell him anything you want, but it's not really his business at all.

He will say that he needs to see your ID, but at this point, you can ask him why he needs to see it, or tell him that he does not. **He will push the issue**. Don't falter. What he says next is usually something along the lines of, "Well, you fit the description of someone we're looking for." This is classic textbook cop shit. Be confident knowing that he has *nothing* on you.

At this point, the cop will tell you that because you are acting suspicious, he needs to look through your bag. There is a good line to use to avoid looking like an asshole and catching a beating while still asserting yourself to that schmuck.

When he asks to look through your belongings, politely say, "With all due respect, officer, there are some embarrassing pictures of my girlfriend in there, and I can't let you see them. If you had a warrant, then at least I can tell her that I had no choice in the matter." The cop will be pissed, but the motherfucker has nothing, *nothing*!

After he pushes the issue, and you continue to refuse, there are four words that you can utter that will give you the relief of being let go. Ask the cop, "Am I being detained?" If the answer is no, then you are free to leave, so do so at a brisk pace. Don't run, obviously, but leave without dawdling.

If you are not being detained, then the cop has no right to search your property or person, they have no right to cuff you, and they have no right to interrogate you. Use this tool to your advantage!

This will not work if you are in a vehicle. If you are driving the car, you are required by law to show your driver's license. Passengers are *not* required to show ID. If you are pulled over, try to be as polite as possible. Do you know of the cliché saying, "you get more flies with honey than you do with vinegar"? Personally, I think flies are more partial to feces, but as far as cops go, be really polite and their attitude should change. Unless you are black. Unfortunately, you are going to catch hell most of the time.

In case you do catch hell, you can fight back by answering only the questions pertaining to him pulling you over, and by providing all that you are required to by law, i.e. driver's license, registration, and proof of insurance. You don't have to show the officer anything else!

At this point, if the cop suspects you of doing what it is that you are doing, he will tell you that he needs to have a look in your car. Here's a quick news flash for you:

He already looked in your car when he came up to the window and asked to see your license. **Make sure you have nothing incriminating in clear view.** It goes without saying, but you'd be surprised how stupid and/or complacent people are.

If the cop does try to search your car, politely decline it. Make sure you loudly, and clearly say, "I do not consent to any searches of me, or my vehicle." This protects you legally in court should they arrest you.

There is something to watch out for when denying the officer the privilege of searching your car or person. He will threaten to get a drug sniffing dog out to your location and often times, he will. This drug dog may or may not smell something on you. It doesn't matter at this point because the officer assumes your guilt based on your reluctance to oblige him.

An officer has been training this dog to smell drugs. When the dog doesn't smell any, it looks bad on that officer. They will do what it takes to make your night hell. Especially if they just plain don't like you. In a lot of cases, the officers will either directly, or inadvertently command the dog to alert. All they have to do is tap on something, and the dog will begin alerting there.

You see, when they train drug dogs, often times they use a toy coated in the drug's scent. The dog doesn't know what it is smelling, it just knows that they get to play with their toy when they smell it. So, when the officer taps on something to get the dog riled up and excited, thinking it's going to find its toy, the dog begins to "alert". This is all the police need to search your car. Try to play nice first, so they don't have to threaten you with the drug dogs.

Let's say these asshole cops show up to your home. How scary is that? You feel like there is nowhere to run, and the only way out is in a hail of bullets. Don't think like that, it's stupid. First of all, you don't have to answer the door for the police. The Fourth Amendment protects you when the police show up.

Let's say you are hanging out at home. You're watching a movie, eating a peanut butter and banana sandwich, or maybe you are jerking off in the bathroom to granny trannies in white silky panties. If you are, knock that shit off. Porn will ruin your dick.

So you're at home, doing whatever it is you like to do, and suddenly there is a knock on your front door. You're not expecting anybody, so you curiously look to see who is there. It's a couple of cops, waiting ever so eagerly to "talk" with you. What do you do?

First of all, **do not open the door**. The police will say all kinds of things to get you to open up. They will tell you that they need to ask you a few questions about someone else, and they will even try to tell you that you are required to open the door to answer these questions. Sometimes, they will even threaten you.

All you have to do is go to the window where they can see you clearly, show both hands (don't have anything in your hands), and keep the door locked. Inform them that your door is indeed locked, and that you don't answer the door for police. Tell them that if they want in, they have to kick the door in.

Don't be afraid, they won't kick the door in. If they were going to kick the door in, they wouldn't waste anytime knocking. If you are being raided, which we will discuss shortly, they will never knock. They will just barge in, usually at really inconvenient times, like when you're asleep. Knocking cops don't have warrants.

If they continue to harass you, tell them that if they want in, they must show you the warrant. Again, if they had a warrant, they would already be inside your house. They want you to open the door so they don't have to do all the paperwork, and reconnaissance in order to procure a warrant. They are hoping that maybe when you open the door, they will hear, see, or smell something they can arrest you for. They will even threaten your children if you have any, but don't be fooled, it's all just a trick.

Eddie, an old friend of mine, was a grower who grew some of the dankest weed in town. He grew it all indoors, in his garage. The set up was quite awe inspiring.

Eddie got a little complacent, and did not realize one of his neighbors was a cop. The nosey cop neighbor saw Eddie throw out a bunch of fertilizer bags, and a carbon filter that was damaged.

This neighbor decided that Eddie *must* be doing something illegal (he was), so he wanted to investigate. He showed up at Eddie's door, in uniform, and the dumbass answered. After a few intimidating statements from the cop, Eddie grew scared. The cop then said, "Look, if you let me look in the garage, I'll forget about anything I may find, and just let you off with a warning. Otherwise, I'll have to come back with a warrant, and you're looking at possible jail time."

So, like a fool, Eddie let the cop inside without a warrant. Think of them like vampires. They can't hurt you inside your home unless you invite them in. **DO NOT LET THE COPS IN.**

The cop immediately took a look inside the garage and saw Eddie's set up. Eddie was arrested on site, and was taken to jail. If a cop asks to come inside, pull a Nancy Reagan and *just say no.*

Usually, after about five to ten minutes of your continuous rejection, they will leave. Take this time to slam a drink, or get high. It can be very nerve wracking dealing with these cock suckers, so take the edge off to keep your sanity. You deserve it!

Unfortunately if the cops do have a warrant, you're pretty much screwed, sans lube. There will be a small army of mindless storm troopers barging through your house, keeping you and your family at gunpoint. If you have a dog, they *will* shoot it, so try to treat your dog well every day before that time comes.

Keep quiet, but make sure the warrant is valid, and that everywhere they are searching is listed specifically on the warrant. If the warrant says "house and garage", they aren't allowed to go through your shed or car. They will, but whatever they find will be tossed out in court (ideally).

Since you are being arrested at this time, it is important to remember your Fifth Amendment Right. This Constitutional Amendment grants you the right to remain silent, and protects you from incriminating yourself. Here it is, listed in its entirety:

Amendment V

No person shall be held to answer for a capital, or otherwise infamous crime, unless on a presentment or indictment of a Grand Jury, except in cases arising in the land or naval forces, or in the Militia, when in actual service in time of War or public danger; nor shall any person be subject for the same offence to be twice put in jeopardy of life or limb; nor shall be compelled in any criminal case to be a witness against himself, nor be deprived of life, liberty, or property, without due process of law; nor shall private property be taken for public use, without just compensation.

Now, there are a few rights granted to you in this one. Most importantly is your right to not bear witness against yourself. In other words, this is your right to shut the hell up. Let's face the facts, at this point, you are being arrested so it would behoove you to keep your mouth shut. The cops even tell you that you have the right to remain silent, but what they neglect to tell you is that you must verbally announce that you are invoking your Fifth Amendment Right. Otherwise, they may try to charge you with obstruction of justice. Just state loudly, and clearly, "I invoke my Fifth Amendment Right to remain silent!"

This right to remain silent also transcends yourself, and onto your peers. What I mean is, don't be a fucking snitch. If you rat on your friends to save yourself, you are a complete scumbag. I almost wanted snitching to be its own chapter, that's how important it is.

Often times, the police will try to encourage you to tell on your friends. They will say things like, "well, you have something to lose, your friend doesn't" or "what kind of friend are they if they let you take the fall?" Don't fall for these traps. Police are dirty, and will employ dirty tactics to get you to snitch. **Don't be a snitch!**

Put yourself in the other guy's shoes. If he got caught up, and the police told him to rat you out and he did, how would you feel? Seems kind of petty to take down the network you worked so hard to develop, just because you're about to wet your pants. That's what a weeny does. Are you a weeny? I didn't think so.

If the time comes for you to face the music, then do so as a man. Not only will you look like an upstanding man to your peers, but you will also feel good about yourself. It's just prison. It's not like in the movies, where everybody rapes everybody, and you get stabbed with sharpened sporks in the shower. There's actually a lot of camaraderie in prison, so long as you stick to your respective race. I don't know why, but racism is still extremely rampant in prison.

Eventually, you will get out of prison, and you will need to go back to work. Do you think the electric company will hire you? Nope. You have to go back to doing the only thing you know how to do to make money right now, and that's being a drug dealer again. It would seem rather foolish to snitch on anyone, knowing that you will eventually have to go back to the same industry, which contains the same people.

If you snitch on anyone in this industry, you will be branded as a snitch, and no one will want to work with you. Now, not only will you fail at getting a legitimate job, but no one in the drug trade wants you around. You fucked yourself royally! And that's if you want to look at it in a selfish way. My biggest concern is ruining the lives of others when it was me who messed up in the first place. It's not that person's fault I got arrested, it's my own fault. I will never snitch, and neither should you.

This is all worst case scenario. Most likely, the police will screw up on some paperwork, and the case will get thrown out. However, you have to make sure you have a good lawyer. A criminal defense lawyer, particular one who usually handles drug cases is what you want. These saints in suits work tirelessly to perfect their craft, so they tend to charge accordingly.

One thing these types of lawyers do is require a retainer. A retainer is money paid upfront, before any paperwork is even filled out. Every penny you spend is worth it. I know a minute ago I said it was just prison, but if you can avoid it honorably, then do so with every ounce of your being. It's easier to run an empire in the free world than behind bars (although there's money to be made in prison, but that's a different book).

Keep your lawyers in the loop of what you are doing, and what has happened. Be honest with them, but never over the phone. Always in their office, in person. They have client confidentiality and can therefore not be bugged, or harassed by the police about your affairs.

If you have a good lawyer, and you are aware of your rights, I don't think you will have to worry much about your arrest. A lot of times, police are all talk, and will try to get in your head. Don't let them in. It's all a big trick.

In review:

Cops are assholes. Remember that these guys are all on power trips. You get more flies with honey than with vinegar.

Know your Fourth Amendment Right. Cops can't just search you without a warrant, so don't let them no matter what they say.

Know your Fifth Amendment Right. Don't say anything to incriminate yourself, in fact say nothing at all except for *I invoke my Fifth Amendment Right to remain silent.*

Don't be a snitch. If you rat a friend or partner out, then you deserve to be ass raped with a cheese grater. No mercy for snitches.

(Side Note): *if you know of a snitch, teach that worm a lesson.*

Chapter Seven:

Security

Once you start moving up in the ranks, and start becoming a key component in a solid trade network, you will need to consider security measures. At this point in your career, people will start coming after you, either to rob you, arrest you, or take your place. Cover your ass.

Aside from the usual PPE (Personal Protective Equipment) you know, such as a gun, knife, pepper spray, etc., you will need to protect your assets. Your assets are your home, your car, your product, your money and above all else, yourself.

At some point in time, you may find that you want intimidating people hanging out with you. You can either just make friends with guys who can and are willing to fight for you, or you can hire people to do this. If they are your friend, pay them anyways, because a friend is more loyal than an employee. Treat that guy good.

In order to protect your money, you will need a safe. Moving it around your house in a small lock box isn't going to cut it anymore. At this point in the game, you have too much money to do that. Invest in a good safe.

You can find safes in most sporting goods stores. These safes are usually made for storing guns, which means most of them are fireproof. This is good for obvious reasons because you are going to start storing your product, and your money in there.

Yes, safes are expensive, but in the long run they are worth it. If you didn't have a safe, you would get robbed. Either someone you know, and is close to you will start dipping into it, or someone will stage a home invasion on your ass. It happens, trust me. So start thinking about security in the home.

Your home is your sanctuary. You cannot let anyone violate your sanctuary, so you must learn to protect it. There are many measures you can take to protect your sanctuary, and some of them are the simplest forms of protection.

Lighting. Lighting is really important when it comes to home protection. When the outside of your place is well lit, it deters a multitude of threats.

Nosey neighbors, or peeping toms will avoid your home at all costs in fear of being caught spying on you. They wouldn't be able to live with the shame from the neighborhood, but that's not all lighting is for.

Burglars are deterred by lighting because they don't want to be seen breaking in. If they are coming for your product, they probably assume you have a gun, and therefore would not want to chance getting spotted by you. There are motion sensor detectors that pretty much come standard for outdoor lighting. While these are great for scaring off trespassers, some are keen to your motion sensors.

These threats know that you have a motion sensor on your lights, and that doesn't necessarily mean someone is up, turning on lights. These assholes will still break in, so you have to have another measure.

Alarms. Home alarms are awesome. If any entrance or window is opened, then the alarm sounds. Most alarms also come standard with motion sensors, so if anything moves, the alarm trips.

Even if the power goes out, the alarm will still work because most come with batteries to last during outages. But let's assume you don't have that model alarm, and your power goes out. Then what?

Dogs. Dogs are nature's alarm. While you have to feed them, and sometimes they ruin your house, they are great to have around.

Not only do dogs make great companions for humans, they also desire to protect us. They will bark like crazy if someone breaks in, and starts walking around your house.

If it is known that you have dogs, people will likely avoid your home anyways. However, in the off chance someone breaks in without knowing about your dogs, they will be in for a surprise. While big breeds may be able to attack the intruder, don't be so quick to dismiss the smaller breeds.

A small breed dog tends to be more on edge, and more tense. These dogs bark like there's no tomorrow, and in usually a very high, irritating pitch. If the dog alerts at night, it will be sure to wake you, unless you're some kind of sleeping freak.

So what if the person knows you have dogs, and they prepare? Well, that can happen. Remember the story about my old friend Roger? I went onto his land and stole a whole bunch of weed from his farm. I did this by giving the dogs meat, covered in peanut butter. It could happen to you, too, so be prepared to take the next step.

Guns. You may find yourself face to face with a crazy individual who really wants what you have, and will do anything to get it. These monsters exist, and in this industry, they show up from time to time. You must be able to fight fire with fire buy using a gun.

If a person breaks into your sanctuary, and they have a gun, are you going to ask them nicely to stop? I didn't think so. Not you, you're a salty dog. **Get yourself a gun and keep that bastard loaded.** I know this goes against all common conception on the subject, but the last thing you want to do is load a gun when you're shitting your pants with a gun barrel aimed at your face.

Keep it out of reach of children, of course, and make sure the safety is on, but you want that weapon near your body at all times. Make sure you are aware of its presence, and others are aware of its presence. This will keep you safer, longer.

When that person comes into your home, waste no time. Ask them to identify themselves if you are unsure if they are friend or foe. Your friends and family should know that you will ask them to identify themselves should they be in your home at night. If the person doesn't identify themselves, or tries to hide, put two in the chest, and one in the head.

A more peaceful way to protect yourself is to live in a gated community. This is a smart way to get along, and most of my bosses in the business lived in gated communities. There are two main benefits from living in places like that.

The first reason is that it protects you from robbers. People are less likely to try and rob you if your home is in a place that is difficult to escape from. While hopping a fence is pretty simple, the psychological factor alone is enough to deter most robbers.

Most gated communities have security guards working on the grounds. This is a very effective tool to use to your advantage. First of all, the security guard is a presence of authority, and will deter most common thieves. Second of all, security guards buy drugs. They are just regular people, and find themselves bored on the night shift, and wouldn't mind having some fun. Hell, you might even get extra security from them.

The second reason, is that it deters police. The police aren't as inclined to believe of nefarious dealings in a gated community. They also won't bother to get snoopy if they're bored. The gate alone is a hindrance.

Your car needs to be protected as well. Make sure you have an alarm on it, and you want to get a sensitive alarm. I know it will always go off, even if it's just a cat trying to get warm in the winter in your undercarriage. But it is better that it goes off all the time, than never at all. If the alarm is sensitive, then it will sound if a cop tries to bug it, or if a rival dealer plants a bomb. Although, that's not likely to happen, but you never know.

Your car is like your mobile office. You will likely have drugs, money, or both in your car. Keep your doors locked, even when you are in them, and never roll your window down more than just a crack. Even if you are pulled over.

As far as far as overall protection, of your money, home, car, and product, you need to launder the money you make. If you don't launder it, the government can seize everything you own, and make you pay huge back taxes or face prison time. **You need to launder your money.**

If you've read my other book, *How to Make Money in Your Spare Time,* then you know that laundering money can be simple. All you have to do is take questionable funds, and make them squeaky clean, hence the term "laundering".

There are a multitude of ways to do this, but it is best to keep it simple. You want to use a mostly "cash business"; A business owned by you that deals strictly with, or mostly with cash transactions.

There are a ton of businesses you can own that usually have these cash transactions. My personal favorite is a fleet of ice cream trucks, or taco trucks, but here is a list to give you some ideas on the next page:

1. Strip Club
2. Bar
3. Liquor Store
4. Pool Maintenance
5. Laundromat
6. Car Wash
7. Handyman Service
8. Smoke Shop
9. Tattoo Parlor
10. Secondhand Store/Thrift Shop
11. In House Stripper Service
12. Stripper Limousine Service
13. Stripper Protection
14. Vending Machines

It's important to choose a business that not only handles cash, but is also less likely to be harassed by governing agencies. You don't want to own a mobile oil change company because you will have to deal with the EPA (Environmental Protection Agency), and other agencies involved with environmental and hazardous material policies.

Be careful with the bar, because you will have health inspections regularly. Don't store anything of illegal nature at your place of legitimate business. Except for the money laundering, keep your two businesses separate.

Now, let's say you own a cash business. How do you actually launder the money? Simple. You just state that the profits you made from drug sales are attributed to your legitimate business sales.

If you made **$250,000** one month by selling drugs, break up that amount evenly throughout the year and claim it as income from your business. If you own strip club, just state that you made that much in cover charges, drinks, food, and of course stage time fees. Now you can cycle that money back into the system without looking fishy.

I've come to the conclusion that the government doesn't really care how you make your money, so long as you pay them their tribute, i.e. tax. If the government is making money, they are usually pretty happy, and will be less inclined to see your red flags.

Recap:

Get a bodyguard. Having a weapon is nice, but having another pair of eyes watching your back is better.

Buy a safe. Store all your cash and product in it, and make sure no one can steal the entire safe.

Protect your home. Get outdoor lighting, an alarm system, some nippy dogs, and a gun. You can't get any safer than that.

Protect your car. Think of it as your mobile office. It needs an alarm, too.

Launder your hard earned money. What's the point of making it if you can't spend it? Clean that money up with a legitimate business.

Congratulations! You now know the essentials of being a drug dealer. With the principles provided in this book, a person can earn a decent living. Don't forget, it's not as easy as it sounds. There is a lot of effort that goes into being a dealer, and quite often you will find that you have no time for yourself. It's a long, hard road, but the rewards are worth it.

Tough times call for tough measures. I'm not judging you. Hell, I wrote this while incarcerated, so I can't judge anyone. The point is that you are not a bad person because you sell people something that they want. Laws don't distinguish character, don't forget that.

You are the kind of person who knows what it takes to make it in today's society. Sometimes, you have to roll with the punches. If you've lost your job, or your savings, what are you to do? Let your kids starve? Let your home get foreclosed, or your car repossessed? Fuck that, you're going to do what it takes. I respect that.

Who knows, maybe someday you will be a kingpin, or a cartel boss. It all depends on *you*.

"Do not go gentle into that good night."

-Dylan Thomas

Check out **How to Make Money in Your Spare Time** to learn other ways to earn cash. Be sure to look for more books by **[673126]**!

Disclaimer

The preceding information within this book is intended for entertainment purposes only. In no way does the author, publisher, or any associates thereof encourage, or condone any acts written within. If the reader chooses to recreate the scenarios discussed, he or she does so at their own risk, and assumes all liability for their actions.

CPSIA information can be obtained
at www.ICGtesting.com
Printed in the USA
FSOW03n1001101217
42253FS